A BYGONE ERA - FLAY DAYS

Introduction

I have long believed that if you were fortunate enough to have a childhood, it probably sucked. As a historian, I know that the fact that your ancestors survived wars, the plague, droughts, ice ages and so many other horrible things, you are indeed a miracle of birth to be here. Complain all you want about how difficult life is but understand that the fact you are here to complain at all is a miracle of genetic marvel. It could be so many other combinations of sperm and egg – in, fact, your cousins (or not) could be here to complain instead of you.

I think my childhood was better than some and worse than others. But you only get one, unless you choose to never grow up. I suppose that still makes one childhood.

I was born to two parents who must have loved each other at one time. The third of three children, I have seen pictures that demonstrate happiness together based on the expressions on their faces and ours. Of course, we all know that pictures may not tell the full story. However, they both appear healthy and trim and involved with their children. During that time, my father was a Lutheran minister, and to my eyes, he looks suave and debonair, and my mother young and beautiful. I'm not sure if she was teaching or staying home with us. She passed away in March of 2018, and her mind was going for the preceding ten years. I'm not sure if any of the things she told me are true.

Many years later, after their divorce (I started to describe it as being "bitter," but I don't know if it was), my father was suffering through manic-depression (today referred to as bipolar disease) and he ended up living with my grandparents and later gaining a lot of weight (this was after I hounded him for years to quit smoking. Winstons – a pack a day). My mother chose to marry her second husband, and move with him to Jacksonville, where they had two more children, my younger brother and sister.

At one time, my two sisters, my mother and I began taking brief summer trips together. My younger sister apparently asked my mother to write a letter of sorts, describing her life, which she did. She gave it to me to read before she gave it to my sister. I experienced my first panic attack after reading that letter. It was quite informative, but it was also disturbing. Around the age of four or five, my father experienced something that took him into a deep depression and pulled him away from any interest in our family. At that time, we were living in Walhalla, SC, where he was the minister of St. John's Lutheran Church. I recall that period of being quite happy, although I did invent two invisible friends, which may indicate that I was in an emotional state of unhappiness or fear when it came to my parents or it may simply mean I was an imaginative child. I have no psychology degree, so I'm unable to determine if that is what was going on.

It was here that my mother began relying on my eventual stepfather, and my parent's marriage disintegrated. My older sister, who died in June of 2016, once told me that she had a therapist who suggested that our father may have contracted an illness that affected his brain. I've no idea if any of this is true or not, but regardless, this is when the marriage took a dive. My father had a mental illness that he did his best to deal with and my mother was what AA refers to as a dry alcoholic. She didn't drink, but her responses were almost always unpredictable, which made for a terribly unstable relationship for me. Many years later, I began to suspect that she may have been undiagnosed Asperger's. She was brilliant, but unable to have personal relationships – not even with her children. My stepfather once suggested she may have had a personality disorder which sounds feasible.

Once my parents finally divorced, my older sister, brother and I went to live with my father at my grandparent's home – a combination house and store with acreage of farmland. I truly believe that this move saved my life or at least my personality. This was in the early 1960's – a time when children of divorce rarely went to live with their father. It made me feel "different," so I developed a bad temper which would keep anyone from suggesting to me that there was something wrong with my family.

This is the story of Flay, as I saw and experienced it. Flay is intrinsic in my bones the same way that the low country and the ocean was intrinsic in Pat Conroy's DNA. If I could only write like him.

For those of you who came in and out of Flay, I hope you'll enjoy the trip down memory lane. For those of you who didn't, I'm sorry. It was almost a mythical place, one that I'll treasure as long as I live.

Flay was the poor man's version of Tara – it was a place in time, and it, too, has now "gone with the wind…" or more likely with a bulldozer. If you were part of it, you will understand the special nature of a store with a house attached and all the people who came and went. If you weren't, I'm going to try to create it for you in your imagination. If you've heard stories from Ted Beam, take care. There could be some exaggerations. He does like to embellish. But he tells good stories.

I went to live at Flay when I was eight years old after my parents were divorced. My older brother, Mark, arrived about six months before me and then my older sister, Noel, came about six months later. We were the only children in our community who lived with our father instead of our mother after the collapse of our parents' marriage. This was quite unusual in the early 60's. My mother once told me that she didn't fight this because she knew we would have family, a house, and food on the table. She wasn't sure at that time if she could provide those for us. She went to Jacksonville with our stepfather. I also believe that the judge in the divorce case gave custody to our father, mostly because the trial, if you can call it that, took place in Lincoln County, where my father grew up. We were related to almost every other household throughout the county.

I've made no attempt to clean any of this up. I just went searching in my writings and included all I could find that I had written about Flay. Enjoy. Disagree. Send me emails – TheMiddleofFive@gmail.com. I'll respond unless you're real nasty. I have three attorneys in my downline. Happy reading.

A Letter to my Uncle Ted – My father's only brother (16 years younger than my father)

September 23, 2006

Dear Ted,

    I know that your birthday is sometime in September. Unfortunately, I have never been able to keep your birthdate and Daddy's separate in my mind. I know one is the 13th and one is the 26th – or at least that is what I think. Regardless, I hope yours is or has been a happy one, surrounded with your grandchildren, your daughters, and sons-in-law, and Sue. You have managed to have quite a successful life with your children, and I am sure you are all delighted with Teddi being back near you instead of somewhere in Florida. I was thrilled to learn of her return to North Carolina, and have recently received several wonderful emails from her. She sounds happy and that is quite important to us all. I hope to speak with her at length soon.

    You crossed my mind this morning as I realized that we were in birthday range somewhere, so I decided to sit and write you about some memories, and to let you know how important Flay was to me. I find it interesting that when I think of my childhood, it is Flay that comes to mind. Almost a mythical place, although it was real, and it holds a major formative importance in my life.

    I remember your dog, Danger, quite clearly. I almost think of her (she was a she, wasn't she?) as my first pet, although I believe she belonged mostly to you. Her bark and her protection were important to me, although I don't think she particularly liked having three new children show up in her home. I do think she adapted, and I can't recall how she left us – what age she was and if she died from natural causes. I just remember her fierce determination to keep anyone from hurting any of us. Was she part Jack Russell? Did they have Jack Russell's then? I don't know the answer to that. Perhaps you do.

I remember meals in the kitchen at Flay quite clearly. The way you mixed your milk, pintos, onions, and cornbread in a glass and eat it all as a kind of cold soup. You probably still do that. It always looked rather gross to me, but that was part of what you enjoyed – creating some shock there for us. I think I have that need to shock others as part of my personality from you.

And the tickling, Ted. I could beat you for torturing me with the tickling. I think I have convinced myself that I am no longer ticklish because of you! How you would laugh. You do have a wonderful laugh. I think I laughed as much because of yours as I did from the tickling.

Remember how you loved to make me mad? People would say I should have been a redhead because of my temper. I have now been a redhead for many years. The temper is still there, but I have learned some measure of control. How much would depend on who you asked. Concerning the red hair, you knew something I didn't.

I want you to know that Daddy and Grandma live strongly within me. I have such admiration for her now, and I deeply wish I could have known her better as an adult. She was a very strong woman, who cared deeply, and I could never see it. Teddi and Angel have been able to help me see what a great sense of humor she had, and it took me years to know how much she loved all of us. There is much I do wish I could change about that, but now I must be satisfied that she knows how important she was to me from her heavenly perch. I wanted you to know it as well.

I know that you have held a grudge against those who hurt Daddy (meaning my mother), and you have done so for years. I want you to know that I do believe Daddy would like for you to give that up. I do speak to him often in my own way, and I think he wants this from you. It is a heavy burden for you, and it isn't necessary any longer. Even with his struggles (or perhaps because of them) he was a great man, an even greater father, and we all know how much he loved us. I am extremely grateful – more so than I could ever say – that I was sent to live with him and all of you at Flay. I think my life would have been severely damaged had that not been the case. I was surrounded by family and friends and love and food – and experiences that I carry in my heart every day.

The campus minister at Clemson (from where I graduated in December of 2006) is from our neck of the woods. He is the younger brother of a class mate of mine. Unfortunately, I have no memory of him from that time – he is 2 years younger than me. But I got to meet with him (his name is Chris Heavner – brother of David in my class), and we sat and shared fond memories of Flay, North Brook, and West Lincoln. He filled me in on some things I didn't know – outcomes of friends from high school. It was such a pleasure to have someone to talk to who knew what my life was like. He even said it must have been interesting to live in the hub of the area – that hub being Flay! I told him I had never quite thought about it like that, but I suppose we were much the center of many things that happened there. Imagine that – we lived in the center of everyone's world. He recalled going to the barber shop where Jim Wilson chatted with the customers with his friendly style. Also, as a Lutheran minister, he knew much about Daddy. That was intriguing to me.

On cold winter days, I can recall the fragrance of Grandma's hot dog chili wafting out of the front doors of the store as I came in from getting off the school bus. I so loved the aroma of her chili. Sometimes it would warm me from the inside out and getting to it to have a bite was like a touch of heaven. I know I could try to recreate that taste (I believe Sue has the recipe) but it just wouldn't be the same. I need the surroundings of Daddy, you, Boyt Baxter, FL Beam cussing loudly, Grandma, Poppop, and all the people who would be in and out of the store. I need the smell of the floor and the huge bags of flour in the back room, and Mrs. Bolick and her lip stuck out with snuff. I need to see Grandma folding her tiny papers or sitting at her sewing machine, pumping out quilts. I learned to sew because of her, and today I make quilts too (rarely). I need to sit at the piano in the house and drive everyone nuts with my repeated playing of chords over and over and over (why did someone not come and scream for me to stop??). I need to see my pinned-up photos of the Monkees all over my bedroom wall.

Sometimes, I just need Flay. It lives on within me strongly, but if I could just walk into it for a moment, really walk in, close my eyes, and simply see all that took place, feel all that I felt, hear all the voices, smell all the aromas – it would do my heart such good. I think I would kill for a can of Grandma's homemade sausage. How I use to gaze at those cans lined up in the basement.

I have tried to write books about Flay. I have written several short stories. I do believe that if I am to be a writer, it is a story that will have to be written someday. But which one? The one about a broken-hearted little girl living through her parent's divorce? Or the one about a happy girl in a happy place, being loved and treated kindly? They are all one and the same, I suppose, and I am deeply grateful that I have them to draw upon. The memories of Flay have helped me to be a much stronger person than I would have been without them. You are part of those memories, and I wanted to tell you just how much I do appreciate you. Thank you for being part of my past that helped me to get to where I am today.

I do love you, Ted. Always have. Hope your birthday was (or will be) wonderful. Do something kind for yourself and be in good health.
With deep love and appreciation,
Lucy

Front Row: Mae Beam, Mark Beam, Edna Sorrels
2nd Row: Noel Beam, Lucy Beam

CHAPTER ONE

I don't remember the first time I saw Flay. My sister recalls going through the tiny town of Cherryville to get there, riding in an old ford (I don't remember the car, but we always had old fords), underneath the walkover that extended from one side of a textile mill to the building on the other side of the road at the outskirts of the tiny town on Hwy 274. The walkover was the way I remember knowing we were close to Flay, that if I could keep from throwing up for about 15 more minutes, I would make it to my grandparents' house. Sometimes I made it and sometimes I didn't. The combination of motion sickness in the old Ford and the exhaust fumes of leaded gasoline, in addition to my father's cigarette smoke usually did me in. But once we passed under the walkover, in which we never saw anyone walking, I was almost home free. More to the point, the other passengers in the car were.

I don't know if I truly remember those moments. I believe I do. Sometimes when your siblings describe a scene often enough, you think you remember. You can even "see" the memory created by another person's recollection. But I'm not sure it was ever my memory. Much like I know I don't remember sitting at the top of the stairs to the attic in our home in Brevard, NC (it was where we lived for a couple of years while my father was the minister at the Lutheran Church of the Good Shepherd). Or was it Hendersonville, NC? Regardless, I can see it in my mind's eye as if I really do remember it. Trick is that I can't. I saw a photograph once. The three of us – Mark, Noel, and I – sitting at the top of the stairs. I think I remember that. I must have only been two or three years old.

I do remember some things in Walhalla, South Carolina. I was about four or five. I had imaginary friends. Do children still have those? One of my friends was named Socky. No idea where the name came from. Another imaginary friend was a woman in the military. She wore a uniform. I don't remember if she had a name. But she was there, just the same. There with Socky, and when things got too sad at my house, I could play with them. I could salute the military woman. And watch her march up and down the sidewalk in front of my house. I 'm not sure if she did anything but that. I was impressed with her marching, I think. And her military bearing. My father was a captain chaplain in the army for a period. I don't think the military woman has anything to do with that. Of course not.

13 | F l a y D a y s

Aerial shot of Flay

I remember planting a quarter behind the church in Walhalla. My father was the Lutheran minister there, as well. I must have been feeling the pinch of poverty because right there between the church and the graveyard – right in front of the storage building – right in front of God and everybody, I planted that quarter. I checked it occasionally. At least I remember checking it once. To see if money would grow. I knew about roots. I wondered if that quarter could grow roots and I would no longer be afraid of being poor. Funny, I don't remember being poor. That came later, when I realized that I had less than others did. But in Walhalla, I had a family and there were lots of little kids who lived in my neighborhood. I don't remember being lonely then. That came later too.

I remember cutting my hair while living in Walhalla. I have always liked to cut my own hair. I suppose that my hair needed to be cut, and it was bothering me. I decided to cut a tiny piece from one side. Not noticeable to anyone, I was certain of that. Except it was noticeable to my mother and probably not tiny. Whack. Wasn't a good idea to cut my hair. I would have to wait to grow up before I could do that again. I would also have to wait to grow up until I could cuss. My mother cussed like a sailor. Do sailors cuss that much? I had to wash my mouth out once when I was four while attending kindergarten in Walhalla. Someone else cussed, and we all had to wash our mouths out. I remember being held up to the sink by one of the boys, who was a good deal bigger than I was. That thrilled me. To be held by a boy much bigger. The soap wasn't so thrilling.

Walhalla was a turning point in my life. Probably because it was here that my mother met my stepfather. Where she taught him in high school. Walhalla was also where my father became ill. Depressed. Which one came first? My father's illness or my mother's relationship with my future stepfather? I want to believe it was the illness. My father's manic depression and his schizophrenia drove my mother into the arms of another man. My dad is not here to ask. I'm not convinced I would ask. But I could ask him about life in Walhalla. I could ask him what his favorite memories were. I could ask him about the many people who came to his much-too-early funeral from this little town in South Carolina. I wonder what he would say. Would he tell me about the family who had a cabin on a lake with canoes? Would he tell me about the women of the congregation who thought he could do no wrong? Would he remember that I had a terrible nightmare here, one I can still recall, with a witch and

Frankenstein? Or would he only remember the very sad things that happened here. I don't know the answers to these questions.

I waited a very long time to write about this. I don't want to hurt people who are still living. I didn't want to cause my mother more pain. Her life has been hard enough. She had a mother who chose to disengage from her life because my mother divorced my father. My grandmother divorced her own first husband. What right had she to judge my mother? My mother, who took my grandparents in, who cared for her brother when my grandmother couldn't do it, who stayed with her brother when my grandfather could find no work and the two of them were put into a home while my grandparents sought employment? What right has she to judge? What right have I? None. We all do the best we can at the time. I must believe that. My mother died this year, 2018, in March. I can't hurt her with this book.

One's background can be so convoluted, filled with anguish and confusion. I have said that anyone who claims to have had a wonderful childhood is in denial. Is it just me who is in denial? I think mine was no harder and no easier than most, but it was mine. I think its past time that I begin recalling the fun memories. Going to my brother's football games with a car full of people and a quilt for everyone's legs because it often took thirty minutes for the car to warm up and by that time, we had often arrived at the game. Going on hayrides and getting my first kiss. Playing with new puppies beside of Flay. Going with the new puppies to run in the fields up the hill behind Flay where there were lots of cows. Putting in a Putt-Putt course we built in the backyard and charging 50 cents to play. Finding out I just mowed down all the turnip greens while trying to create a football field. Okay – that one was not so much fun.

Confusion seems to be the feeling which I experienced most in my childhood. I have likely told my children too much because I was confused and uninformed as a child. I never wanted my children to wonder what in the hell was going on. I have no idea how successful I was or if I failed miserably. Based on my oldest sons and their responses to life, I both succeeded and failed. My second and third son have the distinct childhood advantage of having two involved parents. From my perspective, these two sons have been allowed to become who they were meant to be. That comes with the territory of being a secure child. Nature vs. nurture. My oldest son is getting there with the love of a fabulous woman. I think my personality developed because of a huge nurture – or lack of – in response to my nature. I will elaborate as I go along. Essentially, I believe both are very important, but one side can weigh heavily on a child's development depending on the environment and the care given to a child. Warning: My philosophical side will show up on occasion.

I raised myself. Not a good thing in the best of situations but I don't think I turned out so badly. But there it is. When my parents split – wait – I don't know when they split. My father was in Walter Reed hospital in DC after having tried to kill himself by jumping from a jeep. Or so I'm told. That was in Korea. My mother once told me that he was in the hospital for two and a half years. I don't quite see how that is possible. She's gone now. I'm not sure I trust the information she shared because the timing doesn't fit. But the fact remains that I'm not sure when their marriage ended.

We were living in Columbia – the second time around. We had formerly lived in Columbia, SC, while my father attended theology school. I don't think my father was there, although I have vague memories of a tall dark man. Didn't have to be my dad. I was six years old. There were moments of great happiness there. Andy was born there. My younger brother. Turns out Andy is not my full brother. I've never understood that half sibling thing. Either they are, or they aren't your brother or sister. But neither is my stepfather tall and dark. Andy is my beloved brother. My first child, in a sense. I love him to pieces. He is the son of my stepfather who comforted my mother while my father was in Korea. It isn't my place to judge.

When we lived in Columbia, my stepfather was in college at USC. He had to be a freshman, perhaps a sophomore. I was six, so my mom was in her early 30's. I think she was 26 when I was born, meaning she was 32 when he was 18 or 19. What attracts a beautiful woman in her early 30's to a man who is barely a man? Yeah, I get that part. Kind of. Younger men have never done much for me. Then again, I wasn't married to a manic-depressive man who was a patient in a mental ward and who was sending letters to my mom with daggers and dripping blood. Those were the stories my mother told me. Daggers and dripping blood drawn by my father in letters to my mother. That can't possibly do much for a marriage.

My great grandmother (in the middle)

When I was a teenager, my father told me that his grandmother and Aunt (my beloved Aunt Edna) punished him by putting him in a closet in which they had hung knives. As a teenager, I believed these stories. I thought that those evil women who disciplined my father had damaged him deeply. It was years before I questioned my father's memories. He chose to share some of these horror moments with me. Scissors and knives were always a part of those stories. When I later heard about the letters with daggers and blood, I didn't doubt them. My mother didn't keep the letters. Why would anyone keep such awful things? Of course, not to share with the children you had born to this man.

When I went to Flay to live, I was in the second half of the third grade. I don't think my dad was even there. He may have been in Walter Reed. I just don't know. At some point, I became aware that he had been given shock therapy. Maybe I didn't know this until I was much older. But I recall going to the airport with my grandparents, brother and sister to get him. We walked out on the tarmac. No one does that anymore. But we did. We walked out on the runway, and he came out of the plane. I didn't recognize him at first. I'm not sure he knew us. The shock therapy had done its work. The depression was not immediately evident but nor was my father evident. Was he in there somewhere? Somewhere hidden to stay safe? I have never been able to watch *One Flew Over the Cuckoo's Nest* with any modicum of objectivity. I'm not sure which character invades me most. Same with *A Beautiful Mind*. When other people mention these movies, I shut down. Not a place I really want to go. The memories are too stark, too confusing, too much trauma. Yet, I've watched both. Several times. I'm drawn to *Cuckoo* repeatedly. I'm a huge Nicholson fan. Is that the real reason? Do I head down that road so that I can feel the continued confusion that comes forward when I think of my childhood?

Edna Sorrels, Ray Beam, Great Grandmother Beam, Mae Beam, and Essie Sorrels (my great grandmother died before I was born – I have no "grandmother" name for her)

I'm not writing this because I need to relive these times. I know that sometimes people tackle their memoirs out of the desire to leave something of importance to their family. To allow those who come later to have some understanding of what their parents and grandparents experienced. To leave a legacy.

Playing checkers outside of Flay

I want to remember Flay and I want my children to have some understanding of what it was like. This amazing environment which still fills my very being. The essence of Flay fills my veins. In so many ways, I am Flay. I don't even know what that means. I will take this walk and see if I can come up with a definition of what that is, who that made me, how a "place" parented me more than any person ever did, and how that home became so ingrained in who I understand I am that it makes me say I am Flay.

Is it always looking back at the past that makes one think their present isn't so very good? The rosy glasses we like to apply to our "moments" mean that they really weren't so rosy. They just look that way in retrospect.

When I first got to Flay, I don't believe that my grandmother was thrilled that I was there. Of course, she wasn't. Her life had been deeply interrupted by the arrival of a troubled son and three of his children. At that time, we the fourth child, Andy, from our parents' marriage still resided with our mother. It wouldn't be until years later that we would discover Andy wasn't the son of my father.

If our father were so paternal, why wouldn't he want his youngest son with him? I couldn't assume in my eight-year-old brain that he didn't feel equipped to care for such a small child. I thought perhaps he didn't love him. It didn't occur to me that he wasn't equipped to care for me much less a younger child. I could bathe, if I chose to. Wash my own hair. Go to the bathroom. Get into bed. Do some chores. But a three-year-old, as Andy was at the time, wouldn't have those minimal capabilities.

So, our routine was that we would, on occasional weekends, get on the Trailways bus from Lincolnton, and travel the great distance of 30 miles to Charlotte, spend the weekend with my mother and little brother, and then get back on that diesel smelling bus and head back to Lincolnton. I don't have much memory of those visits. My mother has told me that many nights she would prowl the house and investigate beds, crying and missing her children. I never really got the feeling that was true. Seemed like she had taken the easy way out, and eventually headed south to Florida with her new Navy husband, the father of my wee brother who felt like my first child. Eventually my mother and stepfather had another child, my younger sister, Gretchen.

Ray & Mae Beam

I do remember the bus trips to Florida. Being carsick in my father's car on the way to visit my grandparents does not compare to the horrid retching smell of a Trailways bus for a little girl who was easily and regularly carsick. Mark and Noel learned early on these trips to give me a paper bag, install me in the front of the bus, and sprint to the back where they could claim no kinship. Let the bus driver take care of my queasy stomach. Seems like that helped. Perhaps looking out of that large window in the front helped me to keep from being sick.

However, the trip that stands out most in my mind was the trip with our uncle, my mother's only sibling. He had an old green Chevy, I think, with no air conditioning. The old car held our uncle, his wife (girlfriend?) and the three of us. While we were in Florida, my mother gave Noel a parakeet. I think it was for her birthday. Parakeets are generally tiny birds, but like babies, they come with "stuff." This bird came with a cage. The trip home from Jacksonville, Florida, with no air conditioning, a regularly carsick little girl, and a parakeet in a cage was not what one would call roomy. At that time, there were no interstates. The trip was arduous with many stops and turns. We spent a week in that car, a trip that was only one day and one night. My stomach felt like we spent days upon days stuck in that green Chevy with a chirping bird and sweaty skin.

CHAPTER TWO

Flay itself was a fascinating place for my curious soul. I don't think of it so much as a home than an adventure. At some point, I believe the original structure had been a five-room house. The original four rooms were a dining room, kitchen, two bedrooms, and a bathroom. The back porch may have been part of the original structure.

I do not recall ever dining in the dining room. The kitchen held the kitchen table, of course. Here was the spot where those who worked on the farm sat to eat their dinners. Dinner was at 11:00 AM Monday through Friday. Or thereabouts. This was my first experience with "turns" during a meal. We had to turn the table three times during the height of farming. Which meant, sit down, eat, and get up because someone else was waiting for your spot. Dinner (at 11:00 AM) was part of the pay of the farm workers, meaning you sat, ate, and got up so the next person could eat. This was no time for conversation or sharing one's life stories.

My grandmother and Mrs. Bolick, and occasionally other women who cooked country food, presided at the stove where they spent most of the morning cooking pinto beans, making biscuits, stewing turnip greens, frying chicken, flouring and frying country steak and preparing other carb-heavy dishes, serving plates and cleaning up. Whole milk, which had been milked from our one cow that morning, was poured into empty glasses, butter which had been churned from the fat of that milk sat on the table, waiting for hot biscuits and sometimes molasses. On regular occasions, cornbread accompanied the meals and were devoured quickly on my grandmother's table. Mrs. Bolick complained loudly and regularly about the men who came in, scarfed up their food, with no "thank you, ma'am's" to be heard. Mrs. Bolick loved to complain, while her own sons took most of the brunt of her complaints in life. She moaned about Snuffy's shiftlessness, Robert's poor grades, Dan's womanizing. I can no longer remember the names of all her sons. It seems there were seven or eight. There must have been a husband or man in her life somewhere, but he eludes me if I ever met him.

The Bolicks lived in a ramshackle 2-story house that had some connection to my family background. Someone related to me grew up there. All the homes that had held relatives of mine were near Flay except for the Old Home, in which my grandmother was reared. That house burned to the ground while the Bolicks lived there, as I recall. I never heard what caused the fire, but some of those old homes were tender boxes waiting for a small spark. In most cases, the kitchens of these houses were built at a short distance from the home, in order to preserve the rest of the house if the kitchen went up in flames. But these homes were also built without electricity and heat, and once electric lines were installed, so were space heaters which were left on during the night and could easily spark by themselves or light a fire on a shirt or newspaper that was left too close. Usually, the fire department made no attempt to find out what caused these fires. What did it really matter? There was little if any fire insurance, and the people who lived in these burned out homes had to gather enough household things from neighbors to move onto the next wood home, carrying with them the same easy attitude toward fire and the possibility. That was part of life and people dealt with it. Those were the days of neighbors helping neighbors and then trashing them verbally behind their backs. Ahhh, my beloved south.

Flay had an old oil burner which was in the middle room of the house (which may have been part of the first addition) along with various space heaters and not much insulation. The middle room, which was the room I shared with my sister when I first moved to Flay, had so many layers of wallpaper on it that one could almost refer to it as insulation. In a manner of speaking. I recall lying on my bed and peeling back layer after layer, wondering who put this wallpaper up in a house that no one seemed to care about when it came to decorate.

Flay was about convenience and need when it came to furniture and knick-knacks. Dressers lined the walls wherever there was an open spot, and the middle of the room was kept open for passersby. No hallways were ever implemented in the construction of the house. One door opened onto the next room. Each room had at least two doors – some had three – so that you could move from room to room without need of halls. There was no wasted space in a world in which utility was the main decision for life.

As a young girl, the lack of privacy was hard. I was not used to having lots of space, but I was used to closing doors, and keeping people out. There was no such thing as privacy here unless I headed to the local pasture with my puppy and ran as far as I could go. There I could lie down under a tree and watch the clouds move and change and become the most fascinating and bizarre creatures. And my puppy would play in my hair, teasing it, and licking and nipping at my face, and making me feel loved like no other in the world because she loved me best. But then my puppy, Shasha didn't know that the parking lot next to Flay was for cars and falling asleep under a wheel was a sure death sentence, and my father had to come tell me that Sha-sha, that most beloved and protective of all puppies, had gone on over the rainbow bridge, and I was left here without her. Not knowing she was there, he accidentally backed over her. Again, I was left without someone or something that I loved deeply and desperately. Andy was gone, and now Sha-sha was gone. And I discovered that it might be a lot safer not to love. But still I would try. Rabbits, kittens, and other dogs. They wouldn't stay with me, however. Loving just wasn't for animals or people who chose to leave me over and over and over. But I could love a building. A place that kept me warm and where there was plenty of food, and my brother and sister lived there too. Flay would protect me.

Velma, Mae, and Edna – Sisters

CHAPTER THREE

The room next to Noel and mine's was my father's room. By the time we arrived at Flay, the first house addition had taken place. Perhaps the second. My uncle had a room that was back off the dining room. The floor in this room angled downward, which suggested it may have been a porch at one time.

But the best surprise was in my uncle's closet. There was an opening in the floor for a dumb waiter, which for us was a secret trap door that led down into an old basement room that had been long forgotten by my grandparents. I suppose there may have been a washing machine of sorts, the kind with a ringer on it, where someone did the wash. Our washing machine, and eventually a dryer, sat in the kitchen, where the steam from the cooking and the dryer would create the most delicious warmth on a chilly winter day. But the trap door in my Uncle Ted's closet was a dream for a little girl who thought she had been Pippy Longstocking in a former life. Many of my spend-the-night guests slipped through that door into the cobwebbed and spooky basement below Ted's room. I never quite figured out my fascination, because, through the dumb waiter, I then descended into a room that terrified me. However, I can recall slipping into that closet, strictly forbidden by my grandparents and moving clothes so that I could raise the door and fitting myself into the tiny opening. I was a skinny girl but the maneuverings of getting into that small square was a huge part of the fun of slipping into oblivion. I think that I always believed that once I descended, I would find myself in a world of James Bond like beauty, with spies and guns and secrets that would capture me with their mystery. Oddly, I can only remember one time in which I came up through the trap door. That time, I was following other kids, and as I leaned to go into the door in the basement, I accidentally stuck my hand into an open door on our water heater. The shock taught me a lesson that I have never forgotten. Between me and electricity, electricity will always win. I don't think I burned myself, but the abruptness of the shock stunned me, and I have been very careful with electricity since then. Perhaps it isn't so odd that I remembered that.

Next to Ted's room was the original bathroom for Flay. There was a small sink, a small toilet, and a very small tub. The tub had a perpetual rust stain that ran from the faucet down to the drain at the other end of the tub. I fought that stain for years, believing that there must be something that would remove this horrible stain from the tub. Countless amounts of comet were sprinkled and scrubbed on that horrid brown stain. I poured Clorox and filled the tub with hot water. Sitting there, I could see a slight change in color, which would only prove to be a deceiver to me. The water drained, and the stain remained.

The toilet was whole different matter. I do not want to become incredibly uncultured, so I will simply say that my grandmother's digestive system was not what one would want for oneself, although she seems to have bequeathed to me. As memory serves me, she lived on Ex-Lax every night. And she didn't feel the need to clean the toilet. Perhaps she was simply tired of the battle. Perhaps she didn't notice. Sometimes we get so used to our own personal smells, that we are no longer aware of those odors which can offensively assault the noses of others. My grandmother's revenge is that I have inherited her digestive system. Perhaps that is my come-uppance, as she would say, for being the snob I was. I could have, after all, cleaned the toilet for her. Then, again, maybe not.

Next to the bathroom was my grandparent's bedroom. There were two double beds here. I don't recall thinking that was in the least bit odd. They slept in separate beds but in the same room. My grandmother slept with a rag wrapped around her head. To keep out the noise and the light. Today I sleep with a sleep mask. I don't know if my grandfather had any particular sleep habits. Other than that, they both went to bed at dark. If it was dark at 6 PM, they went to bed. 8 PM, time for bed. While they were still farming, they rose when the sun came up. Sometimes in their later years, it was light outside when they settled in for the night. I know that farmers went to bed prior to electricity because – well, because of many reasons. Exhaustion, no light by which to work, their own upbringing, but I could never quite adjust to this fact. Yet, it did give us as a family some privacy time.

Next to the kitchen, which had two walls full of cabinets full of stuff that was often not necessary, was a huge screen porch. We had two huge freezers on this porch, where the left-over dinner from the day before was stored. Other things were here, including frozen vegetables, meat, and fruit. The canned sausage was kept downstairs in the basement, where it needed no chill. The hams were hung in the salt house at the edge of the backyard. On occasion, I would sleep on this back porch. I recall one time when I had lost a tooth. I was sleeping on a roll-away, and I awoke to find that the tooth fairy had not come that night. I knew there was no real tooth fairy, but I desperately needed to believe that there was one. My father came out to find me in tears. He told me to hold on, reached under the bed, and came back with two quarters in his hand. The tooth fairy must have dropped the money under the bed. Or perhaps I had moved so much that I had knocked it out from under my pillow. The tooth was still there, and I knew full well that the tooth fairy does not leave money without taking the tooth. But I played the game because I knew it would hurt my father badly if I let him know I knew he had forgotten to be the tooth fairy. There are many times in our lives, when we children are called on to be the parent and our parents, the child. I think this was one of the first times it happened with my father. It may have been the point at which I switched places almost permanently. I didn't believe in Santa, the Easter Bunny, happy endings, or family safety. I knew what was real, I was ten years old, and life looked uphill from there. In so many ways, it was, but in so many other ways, it became a battle because of my own choices. But at the age of ten, realizing I was now in charge of me and that if I wanted a father-daughter relationship, I was going to have to oversee it, was a heavy load for a young girl.

As I recall, this was also the timing in which I knew about sex. I was in the 4th grade, I knew the "F" word. I knew it well enough to know that when Greg Gantt said it was "funk" I could explain to my friends that wasn't the way it was spelled. My sister didn't get that information. In the 8th grade, she didn't want to hold hands very long with her boyfriend in fear she would become pregnant. When I started my period in the 7th grade, I had already ordered the supplies and picked out the "style" of pad I wanted to use. I don't know why I knew this. It has been suggested to me by friends and therapists that I may have experienced some sexual abuse. I have given it great thought and cannot arrive at any memory that feels real. There are a few people who feel like they may have been a threat in some way to me. Then again, I just can't get my mind around any real memories. The fact that I had little privacy may have been part of it.

The basement was a whole different world at Flay. The size as I remember was huge, but it couldn't have been. Not when I now look at the land where it stood. The room where the dumb waiter emptied was a separate room from the rest of the basement. The most used entry came through the store. At the back wall where the store and the house were connected, there was a trap door. The door was surrounded by a handrail that kept people from falling in. There was a string with a hook. The way to open the door was to lift it with the string and then hook the string to the side rail, leaving the door open while you descended into the darkness. Leaving the door open meant getting yelled at. Now that I look back, I wonder why the yelling. Leaving the door up simply meant the door was open. I can't remember anyone falling down those stairs because the door was open. What you had to do was open the door, prop it with your hand over your head, and close it as you went down if you weren't coming back up anytime soon. The light was operated by a string to pull it on – or pull it off. The pitch blackness into which you descended was bone deep. I can remember praying to Jesus that I would be safe as I descended into the depths of this black hole. Squeezing my eyes shut, I reached out until I could find the string. Once the light was on, I felt safe.

  A bowl set at the bottom of the stairs, and here the feral cats that lived in the basement gathered suspiciously, flitting in and out as someone poured the leftovers into the bowl. I don't quite know why we kept this family of cats in the basement unless it was strictly for vermin control. It worked quite well. Rats were not a problem at Flay. I tried constantly to tame a kitten, any kitten. Often, I came close, but the wildness would creep back in, either because the mother wouldn't allow me close to her kittens or because the inbred nature of these cats was to mistrust humans. I believed at the birth of each litter that this group would have the kitten which I could tame. I was forever disappointed.

  At first, the cats were the only reason for venturing into this part of Flay. On occasion, my grandmother sent me there for the rare privilege of choosing one of her cans of homemade sausage, the stuff of manna. Of all the things which my grandmother made, there were only a few whose praises I sang. One was her blackberry pie, and the other was her sausage. I have no idea what was in the sausage, and I venture to guess that at this point in my life, I would rather not know. But during those days of fried chicken and biscuits made with lard, the homemade sausage would send my stomach soaring. And would also allow me the ability to overcome my pervasive fear of the blackness of the basement and send me happily into the depths. Instead, I learned to love my pets. I started with dogs that had the unfortunate habit of dying, which brought me additional grief, but one I could name and cry over. After that, I went through futilely attempting to tame the numerous undomesticated cats that lived in our unfinished and dark basement where they controlled the rat population. I was continually disappointed to find that the kitten I had lost my heart to, which had begun to timidly trust me, would eventually sense her mother's innate fear of humans, and move back into the sphere of the wild. I made it through the belief that I could prevail with three kittens before I gave up and gave in. It was an interesting lesson for a small girl to learn. No matter how loving or how food-equipped I presented myself, the kittens became cats that had no use for humans other than their nightly meal doled out by my grandmother. She repeatedly told me that they were wild cats, they were supposed to be wild cats, and they would stay wild cats. With frustrated acceptance, I finally believed her although it made me angry that she was right. As an adult I have attempted to tame a few wild men who had the same natural fear of grown women, and I have found the original lesson to hold. Those who are supposed to be wild will remain so. I also tried rabbits for a short period, but like my dogs, they had no natural desire to live. At least not in my grandparent's home.

The thing I hated was when she made liver mush. The odor was so horrible, I would leave the house for days, hanging out at Reba Eaker's house, or walking the pasture. Again, I've no idea what was in it, but the horrible odor pervaded the very essence of the walls and the furniture. Other than that, the occasional plate of chitlins would send me running. If you aren't aware of what chitlins are, I'll let you do the research. There was simply no way I was going to sit at a table that had that in a bowl.

The steps into the basement did nothing to assuage my fear of descending into that dark and frightening place. I thought that it must be a lot like hell was. The stairs were rickety and narrow. They were built from single slabs of wood with no backing and no handrail. As I grew taller, I could grip the frame of the trapdoor for most of the trip down, but while I was still short, I had to trust that Jesus would hold my hand as I trusted him to keep me safe in my descent. That was one of the few times I asked for his help. Once I made it to the bottom of the steps and took three steps forward, I could feel the door that led into the lit part of the basement. Here, I could grab the door handle and quickly enter the one room which felt safe. This room would be the living room for our four-bedroom apartment, which was built for my sister, brother, father and me. This would be my party room when I reached 13, the room of my first drunk after we had moved back onto the ground level of Flay. But first, this was the barber shop for Jim Wilson, who showed up on Wednesday nights for several seasons to service the old farmers and some of the young men who came from several miles around to get their hair cut. It would eventually house my aunt's beauty salon, *Sue-Flay* so named for my Aunt Sue and the obvious location. Too cute, I know you are saying.

Snowball Fights between me and Noel

I am left to wonder where the other rooms had come from that comprised the apartment where Daddy, Mark, Noel and I lived for two years. The outside stairs to the living room were old concrete blocks, meaning the entrance into this apartment felt more like a sinkhole. On occasion, I threw wildflower seeds around, hoping to create some loveliness amid the old decrepit stairs and a bit of a concrete wall. I don't think it ever worked. The windows were part of the original structure, with old iron separations between each pane. Once you stepped into the room, the entrance to the next room was to your right. One closet was on the left, and there were two twin beds for Noel and me. The room was dark with the only natural light in the living room. From that point, going into the two bedrooms and eventually the bathroom was underground. Without morning light, waking up was tough enough in our room. Once you entered the next room, my father and brother's bedroom, natural light could not penetrate at all. Some Saturdays, Noel and Mark would sleep into the afternoon. I could rarely make it past ten, but they could sleep away hours of the day in the depths of the bowels of Flay.

I once found a bottle of grape wine in the closet that belonged to Noel and me. I suppose it also belonged to my dad. I cried for hours believing that my father was an alcoholic. Now that I've had my own battles with alcohol, I wonder where this fit in his life. Did he drink on occasion? Did he need it with all the medicines that were his for depression, blood pressure, heart disease, and who knew what else? Did he need it? I was so hard on him.

I won't ever know the answer to any of these questions. He died when I was 18, a year after I left Flay. A year and a few months. He left me. I'm 64 years old now. I know he didn't leave me. I know that his health was bad, and his self-care non-existent. I know that I had little to do with his leaving. My grandmother thought he left her. My grandfather was clueless. My brother felt abandoned, I think. But he was married to a family he knew well. My sister was on her way into a college career that seemed impossible for me. I had chosen the path of new mother and new marriage to a man I hardly knew. But I was out. I was out of Flay, and the loneliness that had invaded what had once been a lively and alive world. I had escaped into my own misery and poor choices, and I was scared when he died. I wish I could rewrite the note I left in his pocket. The three of us wrote letters and put them in his coat pocket. I vaguely remember mine. Anger and fear and recriminations. How could you leave me? What happens when/if I fail? Where will I go, who will save me, who will rescue me from this terrible choice I have made? I won't always be the angry disillusioned teenager who seeks her own path. Someday I will understand that I can and will learn from others. Someday I will need you and now what do I do? My sad little note was all about me. Not about Daddy or missing him or feeling horrible because I left him to be so alone at Flay. Just about me. I wonder what Mark and Noel's notes said.

CHAPTER FOUR

Reba Eaker in the store. Behind her is the door to the house.

The store itself was the focus of Flay. My grandparents had purchased this store from a previous owner, and interestingly, it was already named Flay. My grandparent's names were Mae and Ray. Too many rhymes. But it worked. And the store worked. In the countryside, many small general stores sprang up. Some stayed. Some didn't. Some were known for different functions. Once my father recovered himself enough to begin to work at the store, he started a credit system. I can remember it now, the metal drawers with the alphabetic listings on the outside, and the individual names on the 4 x 6 index cards. With dates of purchase, amounts, and the occasional payment. I don't know what inspired him to begin such a system. I assume it was his general social conscience that drove him to become a minister. He wanted to help those who had no money and needed to feed their families. Or needed seeds to plant. I don't think we sold alcohol. Based on my response concerning the purple wine I found, I believe I would have remembered that. I also wonder why it didn't happen. The farmers had a tough go of it some years, and white lightning had to have been part of their defense mechanism against drought and bad crops and disappointing children and sick parents. But to their credit, I never saw it. I only knew of one man who came in drunk regularly, and I don't think that I knew then that he was drunk. I knew I was afraid of him; I would leave the store and disappear into the house when he came in, but I never realized he was a drunk. His son has not fallen far from the tree. Drug dealing and selling illegal alcohol became his son's life. What a tragic legacy.

Some of my favorite times were while I was working in the store. The store. It had its own sound. Another part of the growing building of Flay. When we first moved there it was just a large room with a register island, and one row of shelves for the canned goods. Vienna sausages, crackers, sardines, baked beans. My father initiated the enlarging of Flay by one room in the front. The original doors were heavy blue metal. They slammed closed on my hand one day. I looked at my fingers with surprise. That should have chopped several fingers off.

We sold cold cuts and hoop cheese. The cold cuts consisted of baloney and luncheon meat. To cut it, we had to turn on the electric slicer. It could be called a slicer for many reasons. My father admonished me regularly to be very careful. Every time I turned it on, and the whirr of the spinning blade started, I would hear him if he was in earshot. I wonder how many people cut their fingers off with this blade. I was always careful and have the finger prints to prove it. The hoop cheese was another thing. It was delivered in a huge circle, with the smell accompanying. I couldn't quite get into the hoop cheese phenomenon. But regularly customers came who wanted $1/4^{th}$ a pound, or $1/3^{rd}$.

Reba Eaker on the Party Line Phone. The door to the store is to the left of her.

In the fall, my grandmother made hot dogs and chili for sale. I can remember getting off the school bus on a cold autumn afternoon and being lured into the doorway with the alluring fragrance of Grandma's chili. I said earlier that there were only a few things that my grandmother made which captured my taste. The chili was one. In the years hence, my aunt has told me that she has the recipe. I have no need for it. If my grandmother didn't make it, I don't want it. If I can't walk into Flay, listen to the rook players in the back, and take a whiff of the cotton seeds in the flour room, I don't want it. If I can't hide behind the cold cut case and peer into the pot teeming with tomatoes and beans and ground beef (was it roast?), I don't want it. If I can't sit beside the register, and grin at the customers who came to sit in the store because they had nothing else to do, I really don't want it. Flay is a bygone era. Much like Tara of *Gone with the Wind* has disappeared, and the speakeasies of the prohibition period. Those moments in time that brought forth an environment which shaped a child merely through its physical presence probably exist today. But not in the world of Flay. Those now live in my memory and imagination as well as the others who walked their way through it.

These worlds both damaged and saved us. The parts of me that are Flay are both good and bad. I don't hold with people who can only see the positive in their world. Nor do I hold with those who only see the negative. I look for something in between. Sometimes I get caught more in one area than another. Sometimes the bad and the dark grab me and hold me too long. I've been there too long now. But sometimes it forces me to delve deeper. To become more compassionate, more understanding of the struggles which capture many of us. Then it's time to climb up. To grab the root that sticks out of the ground in front of me, and to haul myself up inch by inch, and to know that deep inside me, Flay holds me together. Holds me strong, and loved, and part of something that lives deeply inside of me.

I thought for year that Flay burned. Much like the other homes around it before, it was a tender box. What kept it from going years before, I've no idea. The space heaters, the oil-based heater that stunk to high heaven, the fires in the slaughter pen that came in the fall. But it lasted for years. I was, however, mistaken. It was bulldozed down at some point when it was likely falling in. Flay is physically gone. I have a brick from the foundation of Flay. I have a piece of the foundation of my world. In so many ways.

CHAPTER FIVE

Noel sitting outside in the "parking lot" of Flay. One of the many cats who lived in the basement appears friendlier than most of the others.

The men who visited Flay came for many reasons. Some came to purchase items for their family. Some came to gossip with the other men. Some came to play Rook. To partner with other men in a random game of cards that gave them friendship and connection. Some came to sit out the rain or the snow or the lousy weather that kept them from farming. Some came because they had nothing else to do. Wives and women always had something to do. Wash to hang out. Beans to cook. Children to raise. They came in groups and they came alone. My grandfather was one of those men. I understand that he drank a lot when I was young. Before I was born. My mother tells me stories of my grandmother calling my father wherever they were living and begging my father to come home and put him in bed. My father went. I suppose my parents never lived that far away. Brevard, Walhalla, Burlington. A couple of hours at most. My dad would get in the car, at whatever time of night it was, and head towards Flay. To put him to bed, to help his mother, to leave his family. How difficult those choices are when one must choose between his parents and his wife and children. How very difficult.

My grandfather did not interact with me much. I never liked him, and I didn't feel safe around him. I recall that my father and he had an argument when I was a teenager. I had disagreed with something that my grandfather had said or done. Perhaps he criticized me. It was the only time I saw my father stand up for me against him. He was of course quite solicitous to my dad at that point. I didn't believe it or buy it. I think at best he accepted that we were there because of my father. My grandmother eventually loved us to pieces. I don't think he ever made it over that hump. My uncle and my grandfather had more in common, and my dad and my grandmother were more alike. I once had a therapist suggest that I had recreated the situation of my father and uncle with my own older two sons. Before the third one was born. I never quite got her analysis. My father and his brother were 16 years apart. Two only children. My two older sons are 2 years and 10 months apart. Some therapists grasp at any theory.

Aspects of Flay that caught my imagination were not part of the actual physical presence of the building. One of those aspects was the fields that lay behind and beyond. The road next to Flay – not the one in front – had no name that I knew of at the time I lived there. It was simply the road that went past Bess Chapel Church. It is now called Bess Chapel Road now. Taking a walk along that road took me past three houses, and up a small hill. Before reaching the crest of that hill, I would climb the fence, and take off in the pasture that Greer Beam owned. He also owned Carolina Freight Lines in Cherryville and happened to be the first man my grandmother ever kissed. As a Beam myself, I questioned her sanity in not pursuing that relationship longer.

"Lucy, he was crazy." That was her response, with a long drawn out "a" in the word, crazy. I laughed and asked her what was so different about that. "He shot out televisions." Apparently, a story circled that when Greer was a teenager, he got angry and shot a TV. No idea if it was ever true. But that was her defense. Forget the money, he was nuts. I

51 | Flay Days

wanted to say, and what was Poppop – the name we used for our grandfather. But I remained respectful for once. I'm sorry, Grandma. Maybe you loved Poppop.

The pasture held all kinds of freedom for me. Lush and green, and full of cattle, I would go there when I was too full of people at Flay. Or too lonely for my mother. Or too angry to deal with those who told me I should have been a redhead. I headed first to the top of the hill. There a huge tree offered me shelter and the grass underneath was as soft as feathers. I would like there and watch the clouds overhead, as they shape shifted and floated. Sometimes I felt as if I was the one floating, and the clouds were watching me. Other times, I lay there with my eyes closed, while Sha-sha, or the dog of the time, nudged my head and teased my hair. I would open my eyes and watch the cattle close by, wondering what I would do if I was charged by one. It never happened, but it remained part of my watchful look as I eyed the cows and they occasionally eyed me back. I could walk through the tall grass to the bottom of the hill, and peer into the creek that was sometimes there and sometimes not. If a drought existed, I would search through the rocks that lay on the creek banks. If recent rain had filled the creek, I searched for crawdads, jumping in fear when I discovered one. Sometimes I sat quietly by the creek bed and contemplated the light that flickered through the trees. This was a haven for me.

I was never afraid of being alone in the pasture. For one thing, I never went there without my dog. Sha-sha was an attack Chihuahua. At least in her own mind. Part taco dog and part something else, she took it as her personal mission to keep everyone away from me. At least, if they appeared to threaten me. One of my favorite games was to have a friend smack me – hit me on the arm – and then watch Sha-sha do her stuff. I wasn't afraid to be alone in the pasture because I believed that she would protect me.

My aunt changed this world for me. I didn't understand fear of my fellow man. Even though I had been through a difficult childhood, no one had ever threatened me physically. I don't think my aunt had that safe feeling of the out of doors. One day she came after me. Expressing her great concern that someone – a man – could find me and hurt me, I never looked at that pasture the same way again. Perhaps she was right. Perhaps she was expressing her honest fear of what could happen to a young girl in the 60's in the countryside of North Carolina. Perhaps it was an indication of the abuse she had experienced herself. I lost that haven. I lost my location of safety and freedom that had given me the sky and the clouds and a connection with my dog that I felt nowhere else. I likely would have done the same if I saw a young girl I loved headed off to a field where there was no one to look over her. I can't really say what I would have done. Maybe I would have offered to walk with her. Hold her hand. Find out why she needed to disappear into a 30-acre pasture which may be seen to be unsafe to an outside onlooker. Whatever the reason for her reaction, my safe world on the hill was lost. Where could I go then?

Earlier, I mentioned the parking lot that was outside of the stairs that descended into the doorway of our basement apartment. I need to elaborate on the "parking lot." That would be an exaggeration. The lot was a mismatch of cracked concrete, tar, rocks and gravel. There was no attempt to draw lines to determine where the cars were to be placed. It would have been a joke to do so. Cars pulled in close, backwards, side to side, lengthwise, sideways. Trucks, tractors, and combines would be randomly parked there as well. Wagons, broken down equipment, and trash. Every so often, I would get the cleaning mood, and try to arrange things in the lot to be more aesthetically pleasing. It was a thankless and mostly impossible job. Getting the litter picked up was not difficult, but getting the cans of paint, fertilizer, old pieces of tractors, car parts, tires, left over seed pails, and ever more "stuff" created a constant battle for storage, and who needed what when. There was nothing like pissing my uncle off because he couldn't locate his newest car battery. I learned that cleaning was akin to death, and I began to focus on other aspects of organization.

Each of the three of us had to work in the store. Here I use the word "work "sparingly. Working in the store consisted of helping customers, sweeping the floor, refilling the shelves and the coke boxes, and generally hanging out. Daddy paid me 50 cents an hour. On my best week, I think I made $8.00. I have so many memories from the store. Originally, the store was a large room with one room to the side to the right that housed the bags of flour. Which meant bugs. I hated that side.

Our Aunt Edna used the cotton bags to make pajamas for us. That was also a popular spot for the card table and the endless Rook games played by the bored farmers. On Saturdays, rainy days, and off-crop periods, the men would gather in that room and take their frustrations out on each other by battling to win the game of Rook. Generally, this was a sweet group of men who were kind to me. However, there was one who entered the store as I exited it.

F.L. Beam was a large (read – fat), red-faced man with a loud voice and offending language. He would come barreling into the front door, cursing loudly and blaming everyone else for his problems. He terrified me. When I heard that voice, I was out the connecting screen door to the house in a flash. I did not hang around to hear the language that must have terribly embarrassed my father.

I have no idea what my grandmother thought. She had a great chuckle that she would emit when anything happened that she felt was unorthodox. When I remember my grandmother, I realize how badly I missed out on knowing her well. I was too busy resenting her. She had a great sense of humor. I even missed her funeral because I was out of town visiting my son in Rome. I didn't even know she was dead until I returned. My husband told me after I landed in DC. That was a difficult afternoon. I would have come home early. She had so much influence in my life and I was so ungrateful. Too late now. I've done my best to tell her. I hope she knows. Back to Flay.

When my father returned to live with his parents, he made changes in the store. To the left of entering the store from the house was a long, high shelf. I see that in my memory and I know that created a great place for shop lifting – you couldn't see the other side. The shelves were filled in with wood. I wonder if that was a problem we experienced. I have no way of knowing. I did my own shoplifting – mostly candy, for which I was caught several times. The worst part was grabbing a candy bar and sneaking it outside. Then opening it to find white mold or bugs. I guess that was what I deserved. My father added a front room. The store was located right on the side of Highway 274. When he added the front room, we were then literally on the edge of it. Three gas tanks outside provided a place for cars to pull in and fuel. Once the addition was made, there was just enough room for one car. We were a full-service gas station. I loved to smell the gas and wash the windows for the customers. There was something pleasing about the ability to allow them to see out of their grimy front windows. Sometimes I would clean the back as well. I recall when gas went from .29 a gallon to .34. Wow, you would have thought the world was coming to an end. I didn't understand exactly how poor many of these people were.

CHAPTER SIX

I use the front of the store (Flay) as my basketball hoop.

There was a transitional period in my mother's life when she was moving from Columbia, SC, to Charlotte, NC. During this time, I went to Flay for two weeks in the second grade. I suppose that was when she was moving. I met some kids who I would later know my whole life. One, with whom I'm still connected, returned home to tell her family that my accent needed to be countrified. It has never happened. My memory of those two weeks is fleeting. I sat in a desk that was for a left-handed student. I guess that was all that was available because of my late attendance. I don't remember Flay at all from that visit. What I do recall is the smell of the school, North Brook #1, and the oldness of it. The oily dark floors, the red brick walls, the concrete steps. The kindness of the teacher who would only have me long enough to know my name. I was related to many of the teachers there. I don't think she was one of them. She was a kind woman who made a lonely little girl feel accepted.

After those two weeks, the Mark, Noel, and I went to live with our mother in Charlotte. I don't know where my father was at the time. Perhaps he was in the hospital. I don't really know, but I do know they had not yet divorced. What I do know is that we went to Charlotte, where my mother rented a small house from her father. It was a two-bedroom house. My sister and I had one room with twin beds and built in cabinets. My brother slept on the back porch. I don't know where my baby brother was. Perhaps he slept in the room with my mother. It was a tiny house. My sister and I began school at an elementary school close by, Villa Heights. My brother attended the local junior high (I don't recall the name of the school) where he once tried to bite his tongue off in a basketball injury. I think a shorter player came up under his chin and forced his mouth to close on what must have been a protruding tongue. The blood was awful.

It was here that my sister made her first sugar cookies – out of corn meal. I didn't know I could spit that far. It was here that my mother threw an iron at me. It was here that I got my second beloved stuffed animal – a large black cat with ruby eyes, which my mother surprised me with on the morning of my 8th birthday. I loved that cat. It was here that I slipped children's aspirins out of a little gold box because they tasted like candy. It was here that I feared my uncle, my mother's brother, who was rather greasy and showed up at unusual times to hang out with us. I didn't like him then, or when I grew up. There was just something about him that made my hackles rise, and I found that I would go into another room to avoid him.

Other memories of this little house include the assassination of President Kennedy. We were sent home from school, Noel and I walking along and having no idea of the reason. Perhaps she did, but I was in the second grade and simply knew I was getting out of school. Yet, there was darkness and eeriness about the day that let me know we weren't out for a good reason.

In the summer while we were there, I think Mark had already gone to live at Flay. Noel and I were home and we fought a lot. I'm sure there was a horror surrounding what our lives were like. I don't recall if we kept Andy during the day or not. But we were bored to tears and fighting and getting on each other's nerves was likely a normal thing. Especially unsupervised. I recall one time calling our mother because I was tired of getting beat up. She told us to clean the house and continue working. That way we wouldn't have time to fight. Didn't work. At all.

A nice memory was Saturday lunch. All the leftovers of the week were spread out on the table and we ate our fill. How I loved that lunch.

Then Sundays, brutal Sundays, when were beaten into submission to get us ready for church. The only time I recall my mother touching me affectionately was when we went to church. She would drape her arm around the back of the pew and massage our backs. It seemed so fake. I flinched and pulled away. Love me at home first and then love me in public. I still feel that way.

My mother's father also lived in Charlotte. I refer to him that way because I never knew him. He was a tall white-haired man who would rarely appear at our house. Looking back now, I wonder if he only came to get the rent. He later committed suicide because he was fearful that he had cancer. He shot himself in the second story bedroom of the house he lived in, which I don't recall ever visiting. His second wife found his body. By that time, I had gone to live at Flay. I recall coming back to Charlotte and staying in a hotel for the funeral. My brother, sister, and I were enjoying ourselves. Laughing and picking at each other because we had rarely stayed in hotels. Our mother got angry with us and rebuked us to respect the dead. How could we care when we had no relationship with him? It was no different than attending the funeral of a friend's grandfather.

There is nothing I can say about my mother's mother. I never knew her. She disowned my mother when my parents were divorced. Interesting since she divorced my grandfather. I once tried to contact her via letters, but her first letter in response to my initiating letter was to put my mother down as a loser. I was then nineteen and had not seen her since I was two. Again, interesting that she had no contact with her grandchildren. I threw in the towel rather quickly.

There is little else I recall about my time in Charlotte. I also have little memory of when I first arrived at Flay. I do vaguely recall going to an airport to pick up my father. I have no awareness from where he was arriving. I only remember seeing him emerge from the airplane and having little to say when he got in the car. My grandmother was crying, but she was often crying when it came to my father's illness. I didn't understand what was happening there. I still don't know. Odd that we can grow up and still have little knowledge of what happened in our childhood.

I was nine when I went to Flay to live fulltime. That was 1964, the last half of my third-grade year. At that time, there were seven people living in our house. I went to North Brook Elementary. My brother was already there, but my sister had not yet arrived. I don't think she came until the beginning of the next school year, although I'm not completely sure. I was unaware that my father had been diagnosed with manic-depressive schizophrenia. He returned from being a captain-chaplain in the army in Korea as the last remnants of the US Army were leaving Korea. I think it was my mother who told me he tried to jump out of a jeep while he was in Korea. I once tried to find his records through Walter Reed Hospital, but it was a futile search. I have no idea what the truth really is. I can only respond to what I saw and experienced.

My father, Keith Beam, is holding the child and standing to the left (looking) of Santa. He was a Captain Chaplain in the Army in Korea when this picture was taken.

When I was in the fourth grade, my father came to talk to my class about his time in Korea. He stood to the side of the room and had a long conversation with someone who wasn't there. Shame filled me. I am now filled with shame because I felt that way. But I was eleven years old – not old enough to know or understand the mental illness of my beloved father. I didn't ask him to come to school again. It was simply too terrifying for me to consider. One of the other students began making fun of him. I threatened to beat her up. I think this is when I began to discover that a terrible temper could sometimes control people. I've spent a lifetime trying to unlearn that.

In the first days of living at Flay, Noel and I shared bunk beds in the middle bedroom. The corner of the room had built in shelves and on these were my grandmother's porcelain dolls, which we were warned not to touch, as well as my father's carved figures. The dolls were elusive. I was afraid I would break them. The carved figures fascinated me. An Army Captain, a minister, several others which I have forgotten now. My father whittled away his troubles and produced the most amazing little people. What I would give to have one of those now. They spoke to me with their tiny eyes and their flat bases foreshadowing the toy story movies. I was convinced that each night, after I slept, they rose and played around our room. Occasionally, in the morning, I would glance suspiciously toward the shelf where they stood to see if they had moved during the night. I could never tell but it looked possible.

This room held an ancient oil heater that still functioned. I deeply hated the smell and the fact that the heat only stayed close to the heater. I woke at night with grease oozing off my face. The corners of the room and the next room were always freezing. Oil heat did not penetrate the rest of the house. Consequently, we had many free-standing electric heaters that were equally ineffective. I either felt cold from a foot away or smothered in damp heat because I was too close. Many homes burned there because of faulty electric space heaters. With the ancient parchment layers of wallpaper, I'm amazed that we never found ourselves blazing in the middle of the night.

My father's room was next door – there was a door leading right to it. At some point, the bunk beds were placed in his room right next to that door. That may have been when Noel arrived, and Mark was in the room I earlier described. That makes more sense logically. Later, three rooms were added onto Flay. One was a living room next to the room with the oil heater. The second room was a bedroom, in which Noel and I eventually stayed, until she left, and it became mine. The last room was a very small bathroom with a shower. The shower eked with black mold and rust. I recall sliding into the opening without touching anything except the knobs for water. Squeezing my body into a straight line, I emerged from the shower, again without touching anything. That was a relatively easy task – I was skinny. The toilet sat on the right as you entered the bathroom. This toilet was relatively responsive to cleaning, not that it happened a lot. Unlike the one in my grandmother's bathroom, which reeked of body waste and rust, this one would become somewhat white with enough effort. The sink was small, and counter top smaller. A mirrored box sat above the sink, with black scratches. Our toiletries littered the top of the small counter. Towels were thin and damp. I never knew any of this. It was life at Flay. I recall, at the age of eleven, my sister asked me to come to the bathroom. I sat on the toilet while she began to tell me about how a woman's body changes. Stopping her, I held my hand up.

"I know all about this," I stated calmly. I was an aficionado of the teen magazines.

"How could you?" She stared me in disbelief.

"I've already ordered samples of kotex and the size and style I want. Along with the belt." In those days, we wore the awful elastic belts that hooked to the end of the napkins. The magazines had ads that sent the samples out in brown packaging suggesting it may be shameful what the female body goes through. Noel sat on the counter, looking at me suspiciously.

"Nobody told you any of this, did they?" At that point, several girlfriends had started their periods. This was a common discussion in our late-night sleep overs. I think I knew more than Noel, but I've always been nosy and asked as many questions as I could think of.

We sat there in uncomfortable silence, she staring at me and me staring at the floor. I couldn't quite figure out what I had done wrong. But jumping ahead was not a good thing. Noel had been thrust into the role of being a mother figure. I didn't envy her that job because my natural rebellious state had to make it quite difficult. Also, we were siblings who fought a lot. How do you become someone's surrogate mother when she's your little sister and a real pain in the ass? There was so much teenage angst that we simply did the best that we could. She did much better than me. I wish I had been nicer and more able to see her as the loving sister she was trying to be. We fought over clothes, food, chores, grades, school. You name it. I don't think we were much different than other sisters, but I know now just how loving she is and I regret not being kinder. We lost her in June of 2016 to Ovarian Cancer. I wonder what she'd think of this book.

Noel & I won the 4-H County Talent Show (I have the long skinny legs and she is wearing the fringe skirt)

From the moment I arrived at Flay, I felt as though I was raising myself. I don't mean this as an insult to my father, grandparents, or Noel. But it simply was the nature of what was going on. My father was ill, my grandparents had a home, store, and farm to run, and Noel was only three years older than me. I had no one to whom I felt I could go and get instructions. Nor was I willing to be instructed. I also learned early that a quick temper and a cutting word kept people from bothering me. My uncle said I should have been born a redhead. The quick temper may have kept me safe in my preteen years, but the same temper years later kept people far away from me. The biting words hurt those I love, and I've lived long enough to regret that and to try to modify the response. Additionally, every person in that house had their own demons with which to deal. I'm sure that is true of most houses. But I didn't live in other places. My father was drowning in mental illness with the ineffective and incapacitating drugs of the day. He slept a lot, as he continued to do for the rest of his life. My grandmother was dealing with the added stress of three new children, and what in the world do you do with them? My grandfather didn't deal – he just lived his life of rook, farming, and hanging out with the farmers. My uncle tried his best, but he lived in his world as well. We truly must have put a huge crack in their otherwise regular life.

    Descriptions here would be helpful. How do I describe my grandfather? He was Poppop to us. As I mentioned, he drank a lot as a young and middle-aged man. I'm not sure if I ever saw him drinking or not. I must have, but that memory eludes me. He was about 5'8" with a head full of silver hair. The one existing picture I have is a man with suspenders, with a beer gut and that lush head of hair with eyes of piercing blue. He mostly stayed away from me, and I mostly stayed away from him.

    My grandmother typified the southern farmer's wife. Each day, she wore a dress with a rounded collar. Pinned to that dress was an apron that existed to protect her dress, although thin and unlikely to guard against spills. Her shoes were practical and brown, with stockings rolled down to the top of her knees. She wore glasses, dipped snuff, and sewed some, making mostly quilts. She also crocheted and would sit in the store creating doilies out of tiny thread and tinier needles. The other habit she had that nearly drove me in the ground was folding paper into tiny fans. While she sat, her fingers were moving. Her fans littered the counter top at the cash register, and the trash cans. I used to watch her and then get up and run out of the store in complete and utter frustration. I have since caught myself making tiny fans. It must be genetic. I recently saw my niece making fans during the reading of my first play. I laughed out loud and pointed it out to my loving first cousin, Teddi. She laughed too. I'm amazed. We don't fall too far from the tree.

    Around the store and the house, old coffee cans were placed as spittoons. For the time that my great grandmother lived with us, both she and my grandmother would take a tiny twig, dip it into the snuff can, and place a twig of snuff in their cheek. Every so often, I heard a ping, as they aimed and spit into the cans. You can imagine the area around the can. They weren't expert shots. Truly, that and tobacco chewing are two of the nastiest habits I have ever known.

    There were many around Flay, including my uncle, who stuck wads of "backer" in their cheeks. Since then, I have heard the horror stories of throat cancer that many of these men developed. What a horrible way to die. Smoking was bad enough. Because my dad smoked (at one time) three packs of Winston's a day, I learned early to hate any habit that had to do with tobacco. My father (wisely) let me smoke a cigarette when I was six. I have never been sicker. That did it. He eventually quit, then gained 60 pounds. I don't know which killed him quicker – the tobacco or the weight.

At Flay, we were farmers in addition to being merchants at the store. We grew cotton and tomatoes. That's what I recall. I know I burned tires around tomatoes, hoed tomato plants, pulled "suckers" from the stalks, and picked tomatoes. I hated tomatoes until I was about 40.

Below is a memory from my brother about the tomato harvest.

My (brother's) recollections (true or not – *disclaimer is his*):

We had about 3 acres of tomatoes, about 20k plants. The seeds were planted in cups and put in a hothouse (usually plastic over a wooden frame) in the spring. I believe the cups were made of grass and fertilizer. When the seeds became small plants, each cup was planted in the field. A wooden or metal stake was driven in the ground beside each plant (staked). As the plant grew it was tied to the stake (about 4 times) so the tomatoes would be easier to see, picked easier and you did not step on the plant while picking. Each plant had to be pruned numerous times. That is, the smaller branches were cut off, so the larger branches could produce larger better tomatoes. The plants had to be watered. The fields were always very close to a creek. The creek was dammed, and a pump was installed. The water was pumped from the dammed water through metal pipes onto the plants. The pipes had tall sprinklers installed so the water could get to the plants, like a rather large yard sprinkler. Each pipe was 10' to 20' long. The dam had enough water, so the pump would run out of gas before the water ran out. Seems like it would take about 2 hours for the pump to stop.

Every couple hours or so we returned to the field, moved the pipes from the watered to the unwatered and repeated the process. You picked up each pipe over your head and carried it. Pretty good exercise. So, in a 12-hour day we would do this 6 times. The pipes were heavy (the longer the heavier). I will always remember sitting in the store and Ted saying, "Ok boys, let's go." What a downer. But we usually raced to see who could get their pipes moved first. Then it was picking time. Every other day was picking day. Each day in between was watering day. The crew of 10 to 15 people picked. We wore a sack around our shoulder, walking down the rows, picking the ones that were approaching ripening. The best ones were just turning pink, so they would not be overripe when sold at market. If they were the right size and had no blotches, they were "number 1s". These were the most valuable. You didn't want to get caught messing up a 1.

Usually someone (Ted) would go to the store and bring back sandwiches and drinks for lunch. Ted was the straw boss and would get us started and then kind of disappear. He would do this after lunch as well but would show up a little before quitting time to take us home. He will deny this. We would gather in the shade to eat. Once we had gathered in the shade at the top to the field. The rows were laid out below us with the creek at the bottom. It was a steep hill. Ted had a new black fastback Ford Galaxy 500 with red interior and a record player. It played the records upside down. (Can't believe I remember this.) As we sat there (I was trying to come up with any reason to leave) little Tommy Martin (he will deny this) got into the driver's seat just to look the car. He got out and as he walked away the car started to move. He had played with the gear shift and left it in neutral and no parking brake set. He will deny this. Some of the pickers had already started down the hill to begin picking. Luckily, they had not entered the rows directly below the car. As we began to shout and point the car slowly began picking up speed. Remember no one was in it. I can still see the steering wheel spinning back and forth as it smashed through the plants and stakes. I am sure we were all standing, laughing (carefully) and pointing where the car disappeared into the honey suckle bushes at the bottom. Luckily it did not go into the creek. We all ran down and pulled it out. It was okay but for many scratches.

    After picking, the tomatoes were taken to Flay and graded in the car shed. The tomatoes were packed into bushel baskets according to grade and then loaded onto a pickup truck and taken to Asheville and/or Black Mountain to the market. I never made this trip. Buyers bought the tomatoes for restaurants, etc. I remember one-time Ted returned saying the market price was very high and we quickly graded more to take back.

The tomato business was very labor intensive, and I believe this was one of the major reasons we got out of that business. It was hard to find people for the hard work and pay. Also, the market may have dropped due to competition. I remember one Saturday we were caught up and Glen Eaker asked a couple of us to help grade his tomatoes. I really didn't want to. He paid us $5 for about a half day's work and I thought I was rich.

I was one of the few football players who looked forward to 2 a day football practices beginning in the middle of August. Buck was the other one. When practice started, I basically was no longer a farmer. I did not like 2 a day's much either. I would help some on Saturdays but not much. I found a place to hide and/or be.

Once we attempted to fertilize by building a small tower of wood (about 10' feet or so), put the fertilizer on top with a stick of dynamite, lit the dynamite, blew the fertilizer into the air and let the wind blow it around. I only remember trying this a of couple of times. Don't think it worked to well.

The earlier you planted and picked, the higher the market price. Problem was if you planted too early a late frost could wipe out your crop. Same thing with late tomatoes. A couple of times we burned tires to keep the frost away. This involved getting hundreds of tires, taking them to the field, stacking in appropriate places all through the field and all through the night, staying up til dawn, and lighting the tires so the smoke covered the field just before the frost came. Ted had to constantly call us back to our work because we were constantly running through the field playing one stupid game or another in the dark. But when dawn came you really felt you had accomplished something. Then the whole crew went to Flay to have one great breakfast. Wow that was a dirty job. I'll send more as I think of it (end of my brother's recollections).

I'm delighted that I have my brother writing memories. He generally doesn't – at least to my knowledge. But that helps stir the pot for me.

This is what I recall about picking cotton. I did. At the age of nine. I would go with the whole group to pick cotton. There was a woman named Mildred – a large, loving African American mother of 11 children. I would work hard to pick, but as a skinny little kid, it was quite difficult for me. If you didn't pick 50 pounds, you didn't get paid. If I almost made it – but not quite – Mildred (the mother of eleven) would give me enough to get to 50 pounds. I didn't understand then just what that meant. She may have been taking food out of her children's mouth, but she was such a compassionate woman that she couldn't stand to see me work that hard and not get paid. How amazing. How loving. How giving. I never knew anyone quite like her. All her children went to college and graduated. I wish I had a picture of the clapboard shack in which they all lived. What a truly heroic woman. I don't even know her last name. On occasion, she worked at Flay, cooking and cleaning.

We had other women work there. The one I truly disliked was Mrs. Bolick. Fat, with a stuck-out lip, she bitched nonstop about her sons and worthless husband. Wonder who taught her sons how to behave like they did. There were several who were very kind and helpful – and quite intelligent. That didn't include Snuffy, one of my uncle's best friends. He was well nick-named. He dipped snuff a lot.

CHAPTER SEVEN

Mark became the athletic star of the local high school. This assured him love and devotion along with adulation from my father, grandparents, and uncle. By connection, my sister and I received some of that devotion with the expectations that we too would excel in some manner that would elevate our status and disguise the rest of the troubles of our family. My sister agreeably went along with the plan, and together she and my brother exhibited their collective intelligence and athletic prowess for the community to comment on and revel in. See? Just because they come from a discarded home and just because their father is mentally ill, they are still good children. They are still smart, accomplished, and athletic. We can still be proud of them. God has been good, and we are all reassured.

I, on the other hand, chose another path. Although I was to demonstrate that I wasn't deficient academically, and my own natural athleticism would prevail for the most part, it was my leaving their world that would finally define and shape me into the woman I was eventually become. Of course, that was after I had rebelled in my own way from the goals and ambitions of the community. Or so I thought.

As the youngest transplant into this world of farming and work, I learned that if I got mad enough, I could be seen by those who rarely had time to see me. I also could be laughed at and poked fun of, but it was better than being invisible. I was determined to be seen. Anger is an effective magic marker, and I outlined myself in red anytime I needed someone to know I was alive. I also used it when I needed to know that I was alive.

As a small child, I had developed valuable friendships with invisible friends, and I arrived at Flay with hopes that they would make the move with me. Sadly, I found out that they had no interest in carving a new existence out for themselves, and I was abandoned again. It had been several years, perhaps since I was six, that I had needed their company, but now I was going where I knew no one and no one knew me. There were, however, no invisible friends to be found, and I discovered that I would have to reach out elsewhere. There was not enough privacy for my "friends" to feel safe showing up at Flay because people were everywhere.

Behind my grandparents' house was a slaughter pen that provided me with enough horror and nightmares that I have never wanted to venture into a slasher movie. As I would walk past the slaughter pen slightly higher up on the road which provided me with almost enough distance, I kept my head turned away, my heart pounding that I was even this close. I knew the ghosts of all the pigs that had come to their untimely and murdered demise were there and would show themselves in their gory bloodiness and come after me should I screw up and glance in that direction.

It was only in autumn that we participated in hog killing, so during the other seasons I wasn't quite as scared, but I kept my distance. And as I grew older, I did develop a sense of comfort that I was safer, perhaps because I was physically bigger but also perhaps because they hadn't attacked me yet, so that indicated they wouldn't.

I vividly recall the one fall day that the magnetic pull gripped me, and my head turned of its own accord toward the gruesome scene. There hanging from a meat hook was the slit body of a hog, with all its organs falling out in a grisly tumble. The hooked hog was being pushed by my brother in the direction of the hair filled tub where I'm guessing they did the gutting of the hog, and the scream that formed in the back of my throat lodged there, threatening to choke me with the size of it. The scream stayed there as I ran drunkenly past the open door to distance myself as quickly as I could. I find it surprising and somewhat disappointing that I didn't then and there become a vegetarian. Paul McCartney would be ashamed of me. Later, at some unremembered point, I did manage to make myself walk into this house of horrors (certainly not during the autumn) and see that it really was just a plain concrete room with a filthy floor and an equally filthy tub along with assorted odd tools, such as the hanging hook and some dull-looking saws. Without the blood-spattered workers and the dead hogs, there was not much to be afraid of. Still, I never ventured there while it was in operation.

It wasn't long after we arrived that two rooms and a bathroom were added to the house portion of Flay. There were no plans other than the size of the rooms, which matched the width of the older portion of the house. As such, there were no hallways or private entrances. To get from one room to another, you had to walk through another room, regardless of the type of room it was. This didn't' do much for creating a sense of space for a young girl in search of growing, so I found a way to go inside of myself that would offer me the privacy I needed. I would bury myself in playing my own made-up version of chords on our piano, or decipher and decode all of the songs of The Monkees, which meant that if you were within hearing range, you got to hear "The Last Train to Clarksville" or "I'm a Believer" over and over and over, until every listener understood every last preposition or conjunction of every single song as I wrote the lyrics in my notebook. In addition, I covered our bedroom wall with pinups of Micky, Davy, Mike, and Peter in their various and comedic photographed positions for the teen magazines, which I bought with a madness and fixation bordering on pre-teenage insanity. I was in love with Micky, the drummer. I was devastated when he got married.

My father had become a Lutheran minister. This was after he had rejected the armed forces as well as law school. I wonder how a man who had embraced his world with the church felt about not being cured by God after making the trade? Did he feel abandoned? Cheated? Did he even think God was supposed to heal him? Or was this a truly convenient hiding place? Perhaps my father felt that he deserved his illnesses. I know I have felt that way at times. But to be there, drug through the muck of deep depression, hearing voices that no one else could hear – what was the feeling for my father? Where was the justice? A brilliant man stopped short of any fulfillment of potential.

CHAPTER EIGHT

Mrs. Teenie Beam, who had been my 4th grade teacher, often picked me up on Sunday morning to take me to Cedar Grove Lutheran Church.

I was a little on the uppity side when it came to choosing church going. My grandparents and my father attended Bess Chapel Methodist. That was too redneck for me, too "Rock of Ages" for my taste. I had a vision that I need to be among the better-heeled Lutherans and that if I attended Cedar Grove, with the judgmental and harsh minister who at the time stood in the pulpit and reined with a steel fist over his flock, I would somehow be closer to where my family had once been. This was the thought process of a 6th grader. Wouldn't it make more sense to go with my family to church to feel closer to them? I think, it my immature brain, I thought it connected me more with the family I formerly had, not the current one. I could pretend for those mornings while standing, sitting, standing, and sitting that my life was truly no different that it had been.

Before the divorce. Before the gradual disintegration of my family. Before I came to live at Flay.

So, my precious and loving 4th grade teacher picked me up as she passed by Flay on Sunday mornings. In my memory, I was always waiting on her, ready and willing to enter an environment that did not want me at all. On time for this appointment with a ride to church, this may explain why I have rarely been on time since.

This was a church filled with intact nuclear families and perfect mother-daughter relationships. Fathers appeared to be part of the plan, and I could gaze silently upon a world that had been stolen out from under me. A place that loudly proclaimed that I was the ugly duckling, but which I chose to attend repeatedly, to endure what I felt as personal abuse, until I received my confirmation. I recall being admonished by a holier-than-thou teacher because I uttered the word, "dang," I was strongly reprimanded that this was no different from saying the other word - I suppose she meant damn - and that I should watch my language, young lady. I don't think I was trying to be a lady. And I do not carry fond memories of her. I can see the agitation and disgust in her face even now. I wondered if she thought my behavior was because I was a child from a "broken" home.

I still have the 8x10 glossy in which my best friend at the time and I along with three other "young ladies" are being photographed for our confirmations. Or the moment after. The dogmatic and harsh minister stands there as well with his expression of boredom and dislike. Still, there is a pride on that 15-year-old face that I had accomplished this goal, that I had attained this special recognition that I mistakenly thought would make both of my parents proud. My dad was with my grandparents (or so I remember) attending the small Methodist church. Perhaps there were family members in attendance. I don't recall. But the importance of the event was that I had done it with no encouragement and little fanfare. I had reached this goal, which was shortly to bear little importance to me.

I left the Lutheran church after that. Mrs. Beam was no longer there to take me on Sunday mornings. Or else I had my driving license by that point and was in the throes of teenage rebellion. Who needed church? I still needed Mrs. Beam, but my vision was blurred by the upheavals in my life, and I lost touch with her. It was time to be rebellious, and to battle my way through life and cut my nose off to spite my face teenage years. I did a rather good job at that.

My sister reminded me of Mrs. Beam at some point in the past few years. The warm memories, feelings, and fondness I still feel for her is deeply embedded. She was a beacon in a time of deep darkness for me. She loved me for who I was, and I felt no recriminations or judgment because I did not come from the perfect family unit. I came with the baggage of a mentally ill father, divorced parents, and abandonment issues with my mother, and the somewhat jaded goodwill of grandparents who took me into their home to raise.

A veritable redheaded force who was unable to feel appreciation for much in her life at that point. That has changed deeply. I do appreciate now. I am humbled with gratitude for what so many did for me. That is the lesson of life - if you can appreciate late, do so. If you can do it early, please do so. Thank you, Mrs. Beam. For giving unsparingly and without any reservations to me with a heart that was so full of compassion, so ready to offer love to a lost little girl, so able to allow me to see myself through your eyes. Thank you for simply being you. Thank you from the very essence of me.

Lazy days long ago

The following short story was inspired by Mildred, my grandmother's helper who had eleven children and gave me cotton when I didn't have 50 pounds. It is completely fiction but is likely what she would have done had this happened. I was later told that all eleven children graduated from college. I do hope this is true.

ABSOLUTION

(A short fiction story)

I sat beside the bed, as I had done for the past three days, waiting for some movement, some sign that Miss Mildred knew I was there. Since my daddy and grandma died in hospitals, they had become places of paranoia for me, and I could feel the chills creep up my spine as I inhaled that medicinal hospital smell that penetrated each and every pore each time, I was forced to go inside of one. This time was no different and four nights in a row meant that smell was now clinging to every part of me, soaking into every hair follicle. But I was determined to overcome the feeling of combined disgust and fear and be here to speak to Miss Mildred when she woke up.

"You here again?" At this point, it seemed that most of the evening nurses knew me. At first, they looked at me a little curiously, a relatively young white woman waiting for an elderly black woman to wake up. I only nodded toward tonight's nurse. "She's been awake a bit today, but not much. Only a few minutes each time. You hang out long enough, I'm sure she'll wake up for you." I just nodded again, determined to overcome my disappointment and knowing I was not the only depressed person in this situation. I was driving my husband crazy by insisting on being here to talk to Miss Mildred before she died. I didn't say that to anyone else, but I knew the reason I couldn't give up. I needed absolution.

Joe got home from work each night since Miss Mildred was hospitalized during the past week just in time for me to knock him over at the door, yelling that both kids had eaten sandwiches and there was one for him on the kitchen counter. "Great," he muttered each night. A sandwich wasn't exactly a home-cooked meal, which I knew, but I worked all day, too, so I wasn't going to waste my time too much time on feeling guilty about that. And I wasn't havin the "you could cook occasionally, too" argument that had gotten old.

So, here I sat. And here Miss Mildred lay. I had known Miss Mildred and her family all my life. As I looked at her aging face, I could see remnants of the woman she once was while I was growing up. She was a pleasantly fat black woman who came to help my grandmother at her farm house three days a week. Her ponderous body was part of her personality. I would never call her obese – that suggested an uncomfortable and even ugly amount of weight. With Miss Mildred, it was about her elegance within her excessive pounds. She always looked fashionable, even when she came to do our housework. Had she ever tried to lose some of the weight, I'm sure all twelve of her kids, along with my brother, sister, and I, would have cried to her not to do it. You forgot how enormous she was because it was the way she was supposed to be.

I had never seen her in a bad mood. "Miss Lottie, ya gotcher choices in life. Why you can choose to be an ol' sourpuss or you can decide to be happy. Old Abe said it da bes' way – most folks are about as happy as they make their mind up to be. You can set your clock by it, girl." I usually got this lecture from her when she could see that I was in a foul mood, or probably when my grandmother told her I was, and I would watch her and wonder just how she managed not to be a sourpuss. She was a poor black woman living in the country of North Carolina in the late 60's when there was supposed to be equal rights for the black people, but somebody sure forgot to come tell my neighbors about it. She had a husband, who tried hard to keep a job, but they were few and far between. So, instead, he kept a bottle. She had twelve – count 'em – twelve children that she was working hard to support and educate and teach the right way. The remarkable fact is that every one of them finished college. We never knew quite how they did it. My uncle suspected it was some kind of special colored scholarship available only to them. Regardless, there were twelve who received four-year degrees, and by God, or by Mildred, they did it. I tended to believe that Miss Mildred might be a bit stronger in this situation than even God. She was an admirable woman by anyone's standards.

Hearing the door open, I glanced toward it to see two of Miss Mildred's daughters enter the room. The older of the two, Mary, smiled at me. She had always been the one most like her mother and treated me kindly when I was a child. The younger, Ruth, gave me kind of scowl that I guessed was meant to be a smile. Or maybe not. I scowled right back. It wasn't up to me to figure out what kind of ill feelings she harbored towards my family or me. That was years ago, and I was here because of me now, not my family.

"She been awake since you been here?" Mary asked softly.

"No, she hasn't," I responded. Mary's expression was gentle.

"You know, you could tell me what it is you need to tell her, and I promise I would get it to her. Case she wakes up while you aren't here at night." I shook my head and looked at my hands. "Okay, Lottie, you do it your way. I just don't want you to upset her. We're gonna go. Been here all day, so we were just checking on her one more time before we leave." She glanced at Ruth. Ruth looked fiercely towards me.

"You aren't gonna tell her something that will upset her are you, Lottie?" Ruth tried to whisper, but it came out more like a croak. I could tell they had been discussing my reasons for being here.

"Ruth!" Mary looked at her and shook her head.

"Ruth, I don't really care what you think about me, but I love your mama very much. I'm not here to upset her. Please rest your mind about that." I knew I didn't say it exactly right, but I meant every word of it.

"You better not, Lottie. She's trying to heal up, and she doesn't need any more of your family's problems to deal with while she does." Ruth had spit coming out when she spoke; she was so angry. Briefly, I recalled that Miss Mildred had named her children after Biblical people. Ruth didn't seem terribly Biblical to me at that moment. Mary grabbed her arm and pulled her toward the door. "This isn't the black Jones family being subjugated by all you white Baxter's anymore!"

"Ruth, let's go!" Mary hissed in her direction and pulled her out the door. I watched them mutely as they struggled together into the hallway. I could hear angry words on the other side, but I made no attempt to understand them. This was their fight, and I wouldn't attempt to defend myself against anyone else. I needed my energy for my confession to Miss Mildred.

I heard a soft chuckle from the bed, and I jumped up. Miss Mildred had one eye cracked open, and she was watching me with it.

"Ain't she somethin'? That Ruth thinks she needs to fight every black person's fight who ever lived. How you doin', Miss Lottie?" The words were a raspy whisper.

"Is it okay for you to talk, Miss Mildred?" Suddenly, I was aware of the effort it required

for her even to be awake right now, much less talk. What was I thinking?

"Yes, Miss Lottie, it's okay. Long as I can keep my eyes open. They got me under some powerful drugs that hardly let me wake up. They must be expectin' me to feel some fierce pain." She managed to crack the other eye a bit. "You seen the stump?" Miss Mildred had developed diabetes some years ago, and after many complications, the doctors had been forced to remove part of her right leg, which was why she was here.

"I can't see it, Miss Mildred. You are wrapped up like a mummy on your whole bottom half." I glanced warily toward the stump, afraid it would jump out and force me to see it. I heard her raspy chuckle again.

"Don't be afraid, Miss Lottie. I ain't got nothin' to be scared of. God will help me get through this. I'm sure of that. He's done helped me get through everything else, some a bit worse than this. I ain't afraid so don't you be." I looked at her weary face and her slit eyes, and I could see that she truly wasn't afraid. She had a kind of quiet resignation about her that said she accepted whatever her God would hand to her. And she really did trust that He would see her through. The kind of faith that had always escaped me.

"Now, tell me, Miss Lottie. What you doin' here? Why you been visitin' my room every night? I know you love me, but I know you well on the inside, too. And your body's fairly shoutin' that you got somethin' to say. So, tell me, girl. What you got on your mind?"

I took a deep breath and tried to clear my head. I had come to do this thing; I was determined, so I ignored all the screaming voices in my head that told me to run – run far away. For once in my life, I was gonna make the brave and courageous choice. For once. And I dug deep for the courage that seemed all washed out of me.

"Miss Mildred...", before I could even get started, tears began pouring down my face.

"Now, you hush, Miss Lottie. I don't need you to be upset about nothin'. You hear me? Don't you be cryin' on account of old Mildred." Her voice was a bit stronger, and she almost sounded like her old self. I could tell it was difficult for her even to speak.

"No, Miss Mildred, no. You gotta listen to me now." I wiped my nose on my sleeve and took a deep breath. "I have to tell you this; it isn't about you. At least, it isn't about being scared for you. I know you're the strongest woman I've ever known. This is about me. About a terrible thing I did. But I have to tell you, Miss Mildred. I have to." I took a deep gulp and felt the sobbing deep in my chest. There was a tissue box on her nightstand, and I reached to grab one to wipe the black mascara that was running down my cheeks.

"Okay, honey, okay. You take our time. Miss Mildred ain't going anywhere right now." She continued to watch me, and I could see a tenderness on her face that I had rarely seen on my own parents' or my grandparents'. I was terrified that after tonight, she wouldn't love me anymore.

I smeared my makeup around on my cheeks some more with the tissue and took another breath. I couldn't seem to get enough oxygen into my lungs, which shocked me at how much oxygen a body needed to be truthful.

"Miss Mildred, you remember when I was twelve, and money disappeared from my granddaddy's safe? You remember I know that they asked everybody if they had seen anything. And then, Miss Mildred," a deep sob escaped from low in my chest as I struggled to keep going with my horrible task. She continued to watch me with the same tender expression. "And then…and then…they blamed it on you." At that, I screamed out, threw my head down on her bed cover and sobbed uncontrollably. As I struggled to control my emotions, I felt her hand on my head, patting me softly and lovingly. "They blamed it on you, and they took you to jail. They took you to jail for three days before anybody had any money to get you out." I was crying so hard I could hardly talk.

"Yeah, Miss Lottie, they thought I done it cause I was the only one alone in the house that day."

"They thought you did it because you are black, Miss Mildred!" I screamed the horrible words into her bed. They sounded muffled even to me.

""Thas' true, Miss Lottie. People sometimes can't help how they was raised. I know that, and you know that, too. It don't make 'em bad folks. Just wrong." I raised my head to look at her.

"But, it wasn't you, Miss Mildred. I was in the house, too. I knew where my granddaddy hid the safe key. It was me. And I never said a word. I never owned up to it. I never told anyone that I was the thief. I didn't tell my daddy. I didn't' tell anybody! That you were innocent. That you were the most honest person I ever knew – ever will know. I let you take the blame!" I put my head down and cried even harder. I felt that I was coming apart entirely.

"Miss Lottie, look at me." I raised my head up, but it took a moment before my eyes followed. "Miss Lottie, you precious thing. I ain't always been honest. Once upon a time, I was a young girl who thought that takin' a nickel or a dime from her drunken daddy was part of my due. Yes, I did," she admitted with a smile. "I stole too, Miss Lottie. Maybe that was God's way of teachin' me."

"It's not the same thing, Miss Mildred." I shook my head as tears continued coursing down my face.

"It ain't? Why, surely it is, Miss Lottie. Stealin's stealin. I don't think the Good Lord says that it's okay as long as it's a little thing. I imagine somebody else got blamed for mine more than once." She looked away from me like she saw the memory. "I was my daddy's favorite little girl. There was five of us girls. I remember my brother got a beatin' one time. A whole quarter was missin'. And he had been mean to me. Stealin' anything is still stealin', Miss Lottie. I was guilty too." She smiled at me and closed her eyes. "I always knew this 'bout you, Miss Lottie. I knew it then."

I cried even harder. "Why didn't you say something, Miss Mildred? Why didn't you tell on me? Why didn't you tell my granddaddy? Or my daddy?" I could tell by her slower breathing that the drugs were taking their effect and she was slowly drifting away into sleep again. She struggled for a few more words.

"Because now, Miss Lottie, you have become one of the most honest people I know. And if I had told on you, why then, I would have cheated you out of the chance to be honest. To tell the truth no matter how hard it is. I done the right thing, Miss Lottie. Look at you now." With that, she slipped away into her healing sleep. I cried awhile longer on her bed, and then slowly sat up. I wasn't exactly sure what had happened, but I could feel the tiniest bit of sunlight open inside of me.

    I wiped my face and stood to go. Leaning down, I kissed Miss Mildred on her cheek. I saw the faintest smile come over her face, and then she eased back into her sleep. And, for a moment, I gazed on the face of the most exceptional teacher I had ever known. Perhaps there was hope for me after all.

CHAPTER NINE

The physical description of Flay would not be complete without the Cotton Gin. Around 100 yards north on 274, there was a large tin building filled with cotton cleaning equipment. As I mentioned earlier, I didn't dare venture into this building because of my fear of losing my hand.

However, next to the Cotton Gin was the Cotton Seed House. These two buildings were connected by a wide, long tin tube. When the Cotton Gin was running, the seeds that were being cleaned from the cotton shot down this tube and into the cotton seed house. The more cotton being cleaned, the more cotton seeds in the building.

What was then left was ½ of a mountain of cotton seeds. A bunch of us would go in to the seed house, play cowboy and Indian, get "shot," and roll down the hill of seeds. It felt like rolling down cotton, the seeds were so soft and the hill sometimes almost to the ceiling of the Cotton Seed House. We could spend an entire Sunday afternoon climbing up the hill and rolling down.

At one point, someone installed tunnels through the cotton seeds with old tin, some if it quite rusty. When I now think of crawling through those tunnels, what could have happened terrified me. Getting cut on the rust could cause some major infection. If, for any reason, the tunnels collapsed, we could have easily smothered. None of that ever occurred to us. The innocence of childhood is something we can't recover.

The other haven for play at the cotton gin was the finished bales of cotton. These stood up on the other side of the cotton gin. We could run along the tops, leaping from cotton bale to cotton bale, or we could play hide and seek among the bales, and we did both. Sometimes, if no one else was available, I ran along the bales alone, singing, "My baby does the Hanky Panky" at the top of my lungs. I had no idea what the "Hanky Panky" was, but I knew the lyrics, and somehow it fit.

The cotton side house was also the place where I received my first and only punch in the nosey, resulting in heavy bleeding. My best friend was there that day, and a boy a year younger was also there. They "liked" each other. He kept picking on her, and I got in the way. He took a swing at me and punched me right smack in my nose. Blood spurted immediately. When I looked at my older brother to protect me, he shrugged, and said something like, "You need to stay out of other people's business." I ran back to Flay, crying all the way, and I think mostly because I realized I couldn't depend on my older brother to have my back. This changed as I grew up and he has been there at every major event in my life. Perhaps he was right.

As we all got older, playing at the cotton gin became a forgotten venture, and we moved onto teenager activities. It was so much innocent fun, and I wonder why we left it so easily.

CHAPTER TEN

I've thought a lot about what memories I have of my brother and sister at Flay, and I don't remember many. I find this odd, but factual. I remember watching Ed Sullivan and Laugh In. I recall washing dishes with Noel after supper each night. This was our chore while Mark's was to milk the cow. He once tried to teach me until I figured out that if I learned how, I would then have to take a turn doing it – which meant getting up every morning at 6:00 AM. I politely excused myself from that lesson. A year or so later, someone left a 40-pound bag of sweet potatoes next to the fence. The cow ate the whole thing and died. Mark still protests his innocence.

My interactions with Noel that I remember were conversations when she was trying to mother me. I supported her when she ran for Miss Lincoln County (and won). I went with her when she competed for Miss South Carolina. One of the contestants came back with her to Flay. There had been a contestant who sang a song and swept the stage while singing.

She unknowingly swept dirt onto the judges (I don't think that had anything to do with her losing). I laughingly said something like, "Wasn't that funny when that girl swept dirt on the judges." Noel and her friend were quiet a moment. And then the young woman spoke up. "That was me." I felt like crawling into the basement. I have continued to stick my foot in my mouth for my entire life. I'm a bit more circumspect about it now, but it happens on occasion. I put it down to being just too direct. I enjoy being direct, but it gets me in hot water on occasion.

Other memories include my desire to watch a scary TV show on Saturday afternoons. This was "Dark Shadows" which my friends discussed at school. I wanted to be part of that discussion, but I needed to preface this by saying I have never watched scary movies. Even today if I hear the music that indicates this is going to be scary, I'm turning the station immediately. I read two Steven King novels – **Christine** and **Pet Cemetery** – and I have regretted it ever since. Mark had agreed to watch it with me, so we sat down, and as soon as the show began, he got up and walked out. I screamed at him, but he ignored me. Off went the TV.

I am five years younger than Mark, so we were never at the same school at the same time. Noel was three years older then me. I was a freshman in high school when she was a senior. I suffered (in my own mind) because of the great successes they both were. They were each Student of the year and President of the Student Body. This was a small rural high school in the Piedmont of North Carolina, but this was my world. I didn't think I had a chance of measuring up to their accomplishments. When Noel was chosen Student of the Year, my grandmother casually remarked that now I knew what I had to do. So, what did I do? The exact opposite. I quit school in the middle of my junior year and got married. That would show her. Man, I do wish I was as smart now as I thought I was then.

The End (it isn't really, but this is all I will write on this story. Hopefully, for those who read this and experienced some of it, it will inspire you to write your own memories. If you choose to do so, please send them to me at TheMiddleofFive@gmail.com, and I'll update the book with your memory.)

To the reader: I chose to stop here because I've been writing about Flay my whole life. Many years ago, I believed that for me to write books about other times and places, I would need to get this one out of the way. I have several other stories I want to tell, but I do want this book published for those who have indicated a strong interest in reading it. As I mentioned that I want my children to know about my childhood and how I was raised.

There was much more I could have written, but it's time for me to move on. Again, I hope you enjoyed it, and for this moment, got to peer into a window into the life of those who grew up in the country at a country store, on a cotton and tomato farm. These things happened and shaped me (and many others) into who they are today. This is a part of the old south that has now disappeared – at least for me. I hope it brings back some fond, more innocent memories for those who read it. Certainly, we had our problems. We were poor, but I don't think we knew it. Racism may have been an issue, but I don't recall it. On a farm, what mattered is how hard you worked, how much cotton you could pick, or how many tomatoes you could save. I may have rosy glasses looking back on my childhood. I don't think I own the monopoly on that.

My deepest thanks to you for reading!

Lucinda Jane Beam Bondurant Hoffman
(Otherwise, known as Lucy)
TheMiddleofFive@gmail.com

Made in the USA
Columbia, SC
25 September 2019